ART OF TEA: Meditations to Awaken Your Spirit.
Copyright © 2001 by Osho International Foundation.
All rights reserved. Printed in Hong Kong. No part of this
book may be used or reproduced in any manner whatsoever
without written permission except in the case of brief quotations
embodied in critical articles or reviews. For information, address
St. Martin's Press, 175 Fifth Avenue, New York, N.Y. 10010

Editing and compilation by Sarito/Carol Neiman
Design by Bullet Liongson

ISBN 0-312-28657-0

First Edition: October 2001

10 9 8 7 6 5 4 3 2 1

ART OF TEA

**Meditations to
Awaken Your Spirit**

OSHO

St. Martin's Press

Rejoice in everything,

even small things.

If you start rejoicing,

even a cup of tea

starts having a sacred significance.

Contents

About the Tea Ceremony

All ceremonies and rituals can be experienced on many different levels. A child might just be captivated by the richness of color and sound, while an adult will have some understanding of the deeper meanings underlying all the pageantry. A person brought up in a tradition from childhood will take things for granted that will strike an outsider as unusual or particularly significant. But every established tradition was once a new and revolutionary phenomenon, and every ritual and ceremony has its roots in a singular moment that so transformed the lives of the participants that they wanted to preserve and treasure the memory of it for future generations.

The roots of the Tea Ceremony go back hundreds of years to a revolutionary movement called Zen, which grew out of the teachings of Gautama the Buddha. Zen's insistence is that the spiritual life of human beings in fact has nothing to do with scripture, ritual or ceremony. And that it is only a series of misunderstandings that led to all varieties of "Sunday religion" where matter is viewed as separate from spirit, where the human is inferior to the divine, where the ordinary is distinct from the extraordinary. Even the idea of God, say the Zen people, is a form of laziness on our part, an abdication of the responsibility that is given to us along with the gift of life. The real religion — or the real religiousness, as Osho prefers to call it — is nothing less than making this very

earth a temple, where all the inhabitants are given the opportunity to flower into gods in their own right, whole and natural, with both roots in the soil and wings to fly.

This book is not a how-to manual for conducting a Tea Ceremony according to tradition. The ceremony, like all ceremonies, is just a time-honored container. The content points to a way of looking at life that is as fresh as tomorrow, and as relevant to preparing a bowl of cereal for breakfast as to sharing an afternoon cup of tea with friends. The container is a particularly beautiful one, reflecting the Eastern aesthetic that underlies its tradition. It has been updated here to accommodate the sensibilities and real-life constraints of the twenty-first century. The practical section at the end of this book guides beginners in the Art of Tea through an approach that they can actually use today, without self-consciousness or the need to continually refer to complicated instructions. For the health-conscious, who have heard of the beneficial properties of tea, there is a simple guide to easily available ingredients.

And for everyone, novice and expert alike, there is a rich content of stories and anecdotes told in Osho's inimitable style, along with small exercises and meditations that can lead to a direct, personal experience of the extraordinary ordinariness and simplicity of Zen.

— SARITO CAROL NEIMAN

BODHIDHARMA'S EYELIDS
AND THE ORIGINS OF TEA

Tea was discovered by Bodhidharma, the founder of Zen.
The story is beautiful.

He was meditating for nine years, facing a wall. Nine
years, just facing the wall continuously, and sometimes it
was natural that he might start falling asleep. He fought
and fought with his sleep — remember, the metaphysical
sleep, the unconsciousness. He wanted to remain conscious
even while asleep. He wanted to make a continuity of
consciousness — the light should go on burning day
and night, for twenty-four hours. That's what *dhyana* is,
meditation is — awareness. One night he felt that it was
impossible to stay awake, he was falling asleep. He cut his
eyelids off and threw them! Now there was no way for him
to close his eyes.

The story is beautiful. To get to the inner eyes, these
outer eyes will have to be thrown. That much of a price
has to be paid. And what happened? After a few days he
found that those eyelids that he had thrown on the ground
had started growing into a small sprout. That sprout
became tea.

That's why when you drink tea, something of
Bodhidharma enters you and you cannot fall asleep.
Bodhidharma was meditating on the mountain called Ta,
that's why it is called tea. It comes from that mountain
where Bodhidharma meditated for nine years.

When the Zen master says, "Have a cup of tea," he's saying, "Taste a little of Bodhidharma. Don't bother about these questions of whether God exists or not, who created the world, where is heaven and where is hell and what is the theory of karma and rebirth." When the Zen master says, "Have a cup of tea," he's saying, "Better become more aware, don't go into all this nonsense. This is not going to help you at all."

Preparation

FIRST EMPTY YOUR CUP

A ZEN STORY

The Japanese master Nansen gave audience
to a professor of philosophy.
Serving tea, Nansen filled his visitor's cup,
and kept pouring. The professor watched the overflow
until he could restrain himself no longer:
Stop! The cup is overfull, no more will go in.
Nansen said: Like this cup, you are full of your
own opinions and speculations. How can I show you Zen
unless you first empty your cup?

NANSEN IS ONE OF THE MOST famous Zen masters. Many stories are told about him, and one I have told many times. I will repeat it again, because stories like that are to be repeated again and again so that you can imbibe them. They are a sort of nourishment.

Every day you have to take nourishment; you don't say, "Yesterday morning I took breakfast so now there is no need." Every day you have to eat; you don't say, "Yesterday I took food, now what is the need?" These stories — they are a nourishment. There exists a special word in India; it cannot be translated. In English the word *reading* exists, in India we have two words: one means reading, the other means the reading of the same thing again and again. You read the same thing again and again and again — it is like learning a part. Every day you read the Gita in the morning; then it is not a reading, because you have read it many times. Now it is a sort of nourishment. You don't read it, you eat it every day.

It is also a great experiment, because every day you will come to new shades of meaning, every day new nuances. The same book, the same words, but every day you feel that some new depth has opened unto you. Every day you feel you are reading something new, because the Gita, or books like that, have a depth. If you read them once you will move on the surface; if you read them twice, a little deeper; thrice … you go on. A thousand times, and then you will understand that you can never exhaust these books, it is impossible. The more you become alert, aware, the more your consciousness grows deeper — that is the meaning.

I will repeat this story of Nansen….

The story is beautiful. It was bound to happen to a professor of philosophy. Philosophy means intellect, reasoning, thinking, argumentativeness. And this is the way to be wrong, because you cannot be in love with existence if you are argumentative. Argument is the barrier. If you argue, you are closed; the whole existence closes to you. Then you are not open and existence is not open to you.

When you argue, you assert. Assertion is violence, aggression, and the truth cannot be known by an aggressive mind, the truth cannot be discovered by violence. You can come to know the truth only when you are in love. But love never argues. There is no argument in love, because there is no aggression. And remember, not only was that man a professor of philosophy, you are also the same. Every man carries his own philosophy, and every man in his own way is a professor, because you "profess" your ideas, you believe in them. You have opinions, concepts, and because of opinions and concepts your eyes are dull, they cannot see; your mind is stupid, it cannot know.

Ideas create stupidity because the more the ideas are there, the more the mind is burdened. And how can a burdened mind know? The more ideas are there, the more it becomes just like dust that has gathered on a mirror. How can the mirror mirror? How can the mirror reflect? Your intelligence is just covered by opinions, the dust, and everyone who is opinionated is bound to be stupid and dull. That's why professors of philosophy are almost always stupid. They know too much to know at all. They are burdened too much. They cannot fly in the sky, they can't have wings. And they are so much in the mind, they can't have roots in the earth. They are not grounded in the earth and they are not free to fly into the sky. And remember, everybody is the same. There may be differences of quantity, but every mind is qualitatively the same, because mind thinks, argues, collects and gathers knowledge and becomes dull.

Only children are intelligent. And if you can retain your childhood, if you continuously reclaim your childhood, you will remain innocent and intelligent. If you gather dust, childhood is lost. Innocence is no more; the mind has become dull and stupid — now you can have philosophies. The more philosophies you have, the more you are far away from existence.

A truly religious mind is a nonphilosophical mind. A truly religious mind is an innocent, intelligent mind. The mirror is clear, the dust has not been gathered, and every day a continuous cleaning goes on. That's what I call meditation.

Philosophy has many questions, many answers — millions. Religiousness has only one answer; whatsoever the question the answer remains the same. Whatsoever you ask is really irrelevant, I will answer the same because I have only one answer. But that one answer is like a master key; it opens all doors. It is not concerned with any particular lock — any lock and the key opens it. Religiousness has only one answer and that answer is meditation. And meditation means how to empty yourself.

The professor must have been tired, walking long, when he reached Nansen's cottage. And Nansen said, "Wait a little." The professor must have been in a hurry. Mind is always in a hurry, and mind is always in search of instantaneous realizations. To wait, for the mind, is very difficult, almost impossible. Nansen said, "I will prepare tea for you. You look tired. Wait a little, rest a little, and have a cup of tea. And then we can discuss."

Nansen boiled the water and started preparing the tea. But he must have been watching the professor. Not only was the water boiling, the professor was also boiling within. Not only was the teakettle making sounds, the professor was making more sounds within, chattering, continuously talking. The professor must have been getting ready — what to ask, how to ask, from where to begin. He must have been in a deep monologue. Nansen must have been smiling and watching: This man is too full, so much so that nothing can penetrate into him. The answer cannot be given because there is no one to receive it. The guest cannot enter into the house — there is no room.

Nansen must have wanted to become a guest in this professor. Out of compassion, a buddha always wants to become a guest within you. He knocks from everywhere but there is no door. And even if he breaks down a door, which is very difficult, there is no room. You are so full with yourself and with rubbish and all types of paraphernalia that you have gathered in many, many lives, you cannot even enter into yourself! There is no room, no space. You live just outside of your own being, just on the steps. You cannot enter within yourself, everything is blocked.

Nansen poured tea into the cup. The professor came to be uneasy because Nansen was continuously pouring the tea. It was overflowing; soon it would be going out on the floor. Then the professor said, "Stop! What are you doing? Now this cup cannot hold any more tea, not even a single drop. Are you mad? What are you doing?"

Nansen said, "The same is the case with you. You are so alert to observe and become aware that the cup is full and cannot hold any more, why are you not so aware about your own self? You are overflowing with opinions, philosophies, doctrines, scriptures. You know too much already; I cannot give you anything. You have traveled in vain. Before coming to me you should have emptied your cup, then I could pour something into it."

Nansen was saying to that professor, "Empty your head. I am ready to pour." That professor had not even asked the question and Nansen had given the answer, because really there is no need to ask the question. The question remains the same. Deep down the question is one: the anxiety, the anguish, the meaninglessness, the futility of this whole life — not knowing who you are. But if you are ready to be destroyed as you are, something new will come out of it. Every destruction can become a creative birth. If you are ready to die as you are, you can have a new life, you can be reborn.

The master is there just to be a midwife. That's what Socrates used to say — that a master is just a midwife. He can help, he can protect, he can guide, that's all. The actual phenomenon, the transformation, is going to happen to you. Suffering will be there, because no birth is possible without suffering. Much anguish will come up, because you have accumulated it and it has to be thrown. A deep cleansing and catharsis will be needed.

Empty the cup — that's what Nansen said. That means

A CONSTANT PROCESSION OF THOUGHTS *in your mind makes you blind. You cannot see beyond them, They create a fog. You become clouded. It is just like dust gathered on a mirror; then the mirror cannot reflect that which is. The dust has to be wiped off, washed; the mirror has to be made clean —then it reflects.*

Thoughts are like dust. For example, you are sitting under a tree and suddenly a cuckoo starts crying—but you are absorbed in your thoughts. You will not hear the cuckoo. That beautiful song won't enter you. You are too full of your own thoughts, you don't have any space so it cannot enter you. It is simple arithmetic: if you want something to enter you, you have to give a little space. Your thoughts are filling your mind so much that nothing can enter.

Truth is the ultimate guest. You will have to empty yourself utterly, only then can truth come in. Thoughts are a preoccupation. People who are too much in thoughts remain in a private kind of world. They have their own world of thoughts and dreams and projections and desires. They go on rushing here and there, but they don't look at the trees, the greenery, the flowers, the birds, the people, the children; they can't see anything.

empty the mind. Ego is there, overflowing, and when ego is overflowing nothing can be done. The whole existence is around you but nothing can be done. From nowhere can existence penetrate you, you have created such a citadel. Empty the cup. Rather, throw the cup completely! When I say throw the cup completely I mean be so empty that you don't have even the feeling that "I am empty."

Once it happened, a disciple came to Bodhidharma and said, "Master, you told me to be empty. I have become empty. Now what else do you say?"

Bodhidharma hit him hard with his staff on the head, and he said, "Go and throw this emptiness out." If you say "I am empty," the "I am" is there, and the "I" cannot be empty. So emptiness cannot be claimed. No one can say, "I am empty," just as no one can say, "I am humble." If you say, "I am humble," you are not! Who claims this humility? Humbleness cannot be claimed. If you are humble, you are humble, but you cannot say it. Not only can you not say it, you cannot feel that you are humble because the very feeling will give birth to the ego again.

Be empty, but don't think that you are empty; otherwise you have deceived yourself.

You have brought many philosophies with you. Drop them. They have not helped you at all, they have not done anything for you. It is time enough, the right time. Drop them wholesale — not in parts, not in fragments. Just be, without any thinking. I know it is difficult but still I say it is possible. And once you know the knack of it, you will laugh at the whole absurdity of the mind that you were carrying for so long.

I have heard about a man who was traveling in a train for the first time, a villager. He was carrying his luggage on his head, thinking, "Putting it down will be too much for the train to carry, and I have paid only for my own self. I have purchased the ticket but I have not paid for the luggage." So he was carrying the luggage on his head. Of course, the train was carrying him and his luggage, and whether he carried it on his head or put it down made no difference to the train.

Your mind is unnecessary luggage. It makes no difference to this existence that is carrying you. But you are unnecessarily burdened. I say drop it.

The trees exist without the mind, and exist more beautifully than any human being; the birds exist without the mind and exist in a more ecstatic state than any human being. Look at children who are still not civilized, who are still wild. They exist without the mind, and even a Jesus or a Buddha will feel jealous of their innocence.

There is no need for this mind. The whole world is going on and on without it. Why are you carrying it? Are you just thinking that it will be too much for existence to carry? Once you can put it down, even for a single minute, your whole life will be transformed. You will enter into a new dimension, the dimension of weightlessness.

Wings into the sky, into the heavens — weightlessness gives you these wings — and roots into the earth, a

groundedness, a centering. This earth and that heaven are two parts of the whole. In this life, your so-called ordinary life, you must be rooted; and in your inner space, in the spiritual life, you must be weightless and flying and flowing, floating.

Everybody is pregnant with godliness. The child is there and you have already carried it too long. Long ago the period of nine months passed. You are carrying something in the womb that needs birth, that needs to come out, that needs to be born. Think of a woman carrying a child after the ninth month. Then it becomes more and more burdensome, and if the birth is not going to happen the mother will die, because it will be too much to bear. That may be the reason why you are in so much anxiety, anguish, tension. Something needs to be born out of you; something needs to be created out of your womb.

That which you have carried like a seed up to now can come out of your soil and become an alive thing, an alive plant. But the basic thing will be that if you want it to happen you cannot be with your mind. Both cannot happen simultaneously. Empty the cup. Throw the cup away completely; destroy it.

WATCHING IS MEDITATION. *What you watch is irrelevant. You can watch the trees, you can watch the river, you can watch the clouds, you can watch children playing around. Watching is meditation. What you watch is not the point; the object is not the point. The quality of observation, the quality of being aware and alert—that's what meditation is.*

Action is not the question, but the quality that you bring to your action. Walking can be a meditation if you walk alertly. Sitting can be a meditation if you sit alertly. Listening to the birds can be a meditation if you listen with awareness. Just listening to the inner noise of your mind can be a meditation if you remain alert and watchful. The whole point is that one should not move in sleep. Then whatsoever you do is meditation.

Understanding

HAVE A CUP OF TEA!
THE ZEN MASTER'S INVITATION

Joshu, the Zen master,
asked a new monk in the monastery,
"Have I seen you before?"
The new monk replied, "No sir."
Joshu said, "Then have a cup of tea."

Joshu then turned to another monk,
"Have I seen you here before?"
The second monk said, "Yes sir, of course you have."
Joshu said, "Then have a cup of tea."
Later the managing monk of the monastery asked Joshu,
"How is it you make the same offer of tea to any reply?"
At this Joshu shouted, "Manager, are you still here?"
The manager replied, "Of course, master."
Joshu said, "Then have a cup of tea."

This Joshu story is very simple. It is so simple it escapes you: you try to grip it, you try to grab it — it escapes. It is so simple that your mind cannot work on it. Try to feel the story. I will not say try to understand because you cannot understand it — try to feel the story. Many things are revealed if you try to feel them. If you try to understand it, nothing is there; the whole anecdote is absurd.

Joshu saw one monk and asked, "Have I seen you before?"

The man said, "No sir, there is no possibility. I have come for the first time, I am a stranger — you could not have seen me before."

Joshu said, "Okay, then have a cup of tea." Then he asked another monk, "Have I seen you before?"

The monk said, "Yes sir, you must have seen me. I have always been here; I am not a stranger." The monk must have been a disciple of Joshu's. And Joshu said, "Okay, then have a cup of tea."

The manager of the monastery was puzzled: with two different persons responding in different ways, two different answers were needed. But Joshu responded in the same way — to the stranger and to the friend, to one who has come for the first time and to one who has been here always. To the unknown and to the known, Joshu responded in the same way. He made no distinction, none at all. He didn't say, "You are a stranger. Welcome! Have a cup of tea." He didn't say to the other, "You have always been here, so there is no need for a cup of tea." Nor did he say, "You have always been here so there is no need to respond."

Familiarity creates boredom; you never receive the familiar. You never look at your wife. She has been with you for many, many years and you have completely forgotten that she exists. Have you looked at her recently? You may have completely forgotten her face. If you close your eyes and meditate and remember, you may remember the face you looked on for the first time. But your wife has been a flux, a river, constantly changing. The face has changed; now she has become old. The river has been flowing and flowing, new territories have been reached; the body has changed. Have you looked at her recently? Your wife is so familiar there is no need to look. We look at something that is unfamiliar; we look at something that strikes us as strange. They say familiarity breeds contempt — it breeds boredom.

That is what has become of your wife, of your husband — nothing is left. Because of familiarity, everything has disappeared. Your husband is a ghost; your wife is a ghost with no figure, with no lips, with no eyes — just an ugly phenomenon. This has not always been so. You fell in love with this woman once. That moment is there no longer; now you don't look at her at all. Husbands and wives avoid looking at each other. I have stayed with many families and watched husbands and wives avoid looking at each other. They have created many games to avoid looking; they are always uneasy when they are left alone. A guest is always welcome; both can look at the guest and avoid each other.

Joshu seems to be absolutely different, behaving in the same way with a stranger and a friend. The monk said, "I have always been here sir, you know me well."

And Joshu said, "Then have a cup of tea." The manager couldn't understand. What is this? What is happening? This looks illogical. It's okay to offer a cup of tea to a stranger, but to this disciple who has always been here…?

So he asked, "Why do you respond in the same way to different persons, to different questions?"

Joshu called loudly, "Manager, are you here?"

The manager said, "Yes sir, of course I am here."

And Joshu said, "Then have a cup of tea."

This asking loudly, "Manager, are you here?" is calling his presence, his awareness. Awareness is always new, it is always a stranger, the unknown. The body becomes familiar not the soul — never. You may know the body of your wife; you will never know the unknown, hidden person — never. That cannot be known, you cannot know it. It is a mystery; you cannot explain it.

When Joshu called, "Manager, are you here?" suddenly the manager became aware. He forgot that he was a manager, he forgot that he was a body; he responded from his heart. He said, "Yes sir."

This asking loudly was so sudden, it was just like a shock. Suddenly the past, the old, the mind, dropped. The manager was there no more — simply a consciousness was responding. Consciousness is always new, constantly new; it is always being born; it is never old. And Joshu said, "Then have a cup of tea."

The first thing to be felt about the story is that for Joshu, everything is new, strange, mysterious. Whether it is the known or the unknown, the familiar or the unfamiliar, it makes no difference. If you go to a garden every day, by and by you will stop looking at the trees. You will think you have already looked at them, that you know them.

21

By and by you will stop listening to the birds; they will be singing, but you will not listen. You will have become familiar; your eyes are closed, your ears are closed. If Joshu goes to the same garden — and he may have been going there every day for many, many lives — he will hear the birds, he will look at the trees. Everything, every moment, is new for him.

This is what awareness means. For awareness, everything is constantly new. Nothing is old, nothing can be old. Everything is being created every moment — it is a continuous flow of creativity. Awareness never carries memory as a burden.

A meditative mind always lives in the new, in the fresh. The whole existence is newly born — as fresh as a dewdrop, as fresh as a leaf coming out in the spring. It is just like the eyes of a newborn babe: everything is fresh, clear, with no dust on it. This is the first thing to be felt. If you look at the world and feel everything is old, it shows you are not meditative. When you feel everything is old, it shows you have an old mind, a rotten mind. If your mind is fresh, the world is fresh. The world is not the question, the mirror is the question. If there is dust on the mirror the world is old; if there is no dust on the mirror, how can the world be old?

If things get old you will live in boredom. Everybody lives in boredom; everybody is bored to death. Look at people's faces. They carry life as a burden — boring, with no meaning. It seems that everything is just a nightmare, a very cruel joke, that somebody is playing a trick, torturing

them. Life is not a celebration, it cannot be. With a mind burdened by memory, life cannot be a celebration. Celebration is possible only when existence is a continuous newness, and existence is always young. When nothing grows old, when nothing really dies — because everything is constantly reborn — it becomes a dance. Then it is an inner music flowing. Whether you play an instrument or not is not the point, the music is flowing.

I have heard a story. It happened in Ajmer... You must have heard about one Sufi mystic, Moinuddin Chishti, whose *dargah*, whose tomb, is in Ajmer. Chishti was a great mystic, one of the greatest ever born, and he was a musician. To be a musician is to be against Islam because music is prohibited. He played on the sitar and on other instruments. He was a great musician and he enjoyed it. Five times every day, when a Mohammedan is required to pray the five ritual prayers, he wouldn't pray, he would simply play on his instrument. That was his prayer.

This was absolutely anti-religious but nobody could say anything to Chishti. Many times people would come to tell him so, and he would start singing and the song would be so beautiful they would forget completely why they had come. He would start playing on his instrument and it would be so prayerful that even scholars and pundits and maulvis who had come to object, wouldn't object. They would remember at home; when they were back at home they would remember why they had gone to see him.

Chishti's fame spread over the world. From every part of

the world, people started coming. One man, Jilani, himself
a great mystic, came from Baghdad just to see Chishti.
When Chishti heard that Jilani was coming he felt, "To pay
respect to Jilani it will not be good to play my instrument
now. Because he is such an orthodox Mohammedan, it will
not be a good welcome. He may feel hurt." So only for that
day, in his whole life, he decided he would not play, he
would not sing. He waited all day, and in the afternoon
Jilani came. Chishti had hidden his instruments.

When Jilani came and they both sat in silence, the instruments started to make music — the whole room was filled.
Chishti became very puzzled over what to do. He had
hidden them, and such music he had never known before.
Jilani laughed and said, "Rules are not for you, you need
not hide them. Rules are for ordinary people, rules
are not for you — you should not hide them. How can you
hide your soul? Your hands may not play, you may not sing
from your throat, but your whole being is musical. And
this whole room is filled with so much music, with so many
vibrations that now the whole room is playing by itself."

When your mind is fresh the whole existence becomes a
melody. When you are fresh, freshness is everywhere and
the whole existence responds. When you are young, not burdened by memory, everything is young and new and strange.

This Joshu is wonderful. This has to be felt deeply, then
you will be able to understand. But that understanding will
be more like feeling than understanding — not mental, but
from the heart.

Many more dimensions are hidden in this story. Another dimension is that when you come to an enlightened person, whatsoever you say makes no difference; his response will be the same. Your questions, your answers are not meaningful, not relevant; his response will be the same. To all the three men Joshu responded in the same way because an enlightened person remains the same. No situation changes him; the situation is not relevant.

You are changed by the situation, you are completely changed; you are manipulated by the situation. Meeting a person who is a stranger, you behave differently. You are more tense, trying to judge the situation: What type of man is this? Is he dangerous, not dangerous? Will he prove friendly or not? You look with fear. That's why with strangers you feel an uneasiness.

If you are traveling in a train, the first thing you will see is passengers asking each other what they do, where their home is, where they are going. What is the need of these questions? These questions are meaningful because then they can be at ease. People start asking questions not because they are very curious about you; no, they just want to judge the situation — whether they can relax, whether they are in a familiar atmosphere or if something strange is there. They are on their guard and this is their inquiry for safety.

Your face changes continually. If you see a stranger you have a different face; if you see a friend, immediately the face changes; if your servant is there you have a different

face; if your boss is there you have a different face. You continuously change your masks because you depend on the situation. You don't have a soul, you are not integrated; things around you change you.

That is not the case with a Joshu. With a Joshu, the case is totally different. He changes his surroundings, he is not changed by his surroundings. Whatsoever happens around him is irrelevant, his face remains the same; there is no need to change the mask.

It is reported that once a governor came to see Joshu. Of course, he was a great politician, a powerful man — a governor. He wrote on a paper, "I have come to see you," his name, and governor of such-and-such state. He must have knowingly or unknowingly wanted to influence Joshu.

Joshu looked at the paper, threw it away and said to the man who had brought the message, "Say I don't want to see this fellow at all. Throw him out."

The man went and said, "Joshu has said, 'Throw him out.' He has thrown your paper away and said, 'I don't want to see this fellow.' "

The governor understood. He wrote again on a paper just his name and, "I would like to see you."

The paper reached Joshu and he said, "So this is the fellow! Bring him in."

The governor came in and he asked, "But why did you behave in such a strange way? You said, 'Throw this man out.' "

Joshu said, "Faces are not allowed here. 'Governor' is a face, a mask. I recognize you very well, but I don't recognize masks, and if you have come with a mask you are not allowed. Now it is okay; I know you very well but I don't know any governor. The next time you come leave the governor behind, leave it at your house; don't bring it with you."

We are almost continuously using faces; immediately we change. If we see changes in the situation we change immediately, as if we have no integrated soul, no crystallized soul. For Joshu, everything is the same — this stranger, this friend, a disciple, this manager. With his response, "Have a cup of tea," he remains the same inside.

And why have a cup of tea? This is a very symbolic thing for Zen masters. Tea was discovered by Zen masters and tea is not an ordinary thing for them. Tea is just like prayer. It was discovered by them. The very name comes from a Chinese monastery, Ta. There, for the first time, they discovered tea, and they found that tea helps meditation because tea makes you more alert, it gives you a certain awareness. That's why if you take tea you will find it difficult to go to sleep immediately. They found tea helps awareness, alertness, so in a Zen monastery tea is part of meditation.

What more can Joshu offer than awareness? When he says, "Have a cup of tea," he is saying, "Have a cup of awareness." Tea is very symbolic for them. He says, "Have a cup of awareness. That is all that enlightenment can do.

If you come to me what can I offer you? I have nothing other than a cup of tea."

To the familiar or unfamiliar, to a friend or a stranger, or even to the manager who has always been there managing his monastery, "Have a cup of tea." That's all a buddha can offer to anybody, but there is nothing more valuable than that.

In Zen monasteries they have a tearoom. It is like a temple, the most sacred place. You cannot enter with your shoes because it is a tearoom; you cannot enter without taking a bath. Tea means awareness and the ritual is just like prayer. When people enter a tearoom they become silent; when they enter the room no talk is allowed, they become silent. They sit on the floor in a meditative posture and then the hostess or the host prepares tea. Everybody is silent. The tea starts boiling and everybody has to listen to it, to the sound, to the kettle creating music. Everybody has to listen to it. The drinking has started though the tea is not even ready.

If you ask Zen people they will say tea is not something that you pour with unawareness and drink like any other drink. It is not a drink, it is meditation; it is prayer. So they listen to the kettle creating a melody, and in that listening they become more silent, more alert.

Then cups are put before them and they touch them. Those cups are not ordinary; every monastery has its own unique cups, they prepare their own cups. Even if they are purchased from the market, first they break them then glue them again so the cup becomes special, so you cannot find any replica of it anywhere else. Then everybody touches the cup, feels the cup.

The cup represents the body; if tea means awareness, then the cup means the body. And if you are going to be alert, you have to be alert from the very roots of your body. Touching, they are alert, meditating. Then the tea is poured. The aroma comes, the smell. This whole process takes a long time — one hour, two hours — so it is not just within a minute that you have drunk the tea, thrown the cup down and gone away. No, it is a long process — slow, so that you become aware of each step.

And then they drink. The taste, the heat — everything has to be done with very alert mindfulness. That's why the master gives the tea to the disciple. With a master pouring tea in your cup you will be more alert and aware. With a servant pouring tea in your cup you can simply forget him. When Joshu pours tea in your cup — if I come and pour tea in your cup — your mind will stop, you will be silent. Something special is happening, something sacred. Tea becomes a meditation.

Joshu said to all three men, "Have a cup of tea." Tea was just an excuse. Joshu will give them more awareness, and awareness comes through sensitivity. You have to be more sensitive whatsoever you do, so even a trivial thing like tea... Can you find anything more trivial than tea? Can you find anything more lowly, more ordinary than tea? No, you cannot. And Zen monks and masters have

CREATE A DISTANCE

between the noise of your head and your being.
Move as far away from the head as possible.
The farther you are away from the head the better
because from that extreme
you will not be able to hear the noise of the head.
Slowly, slowly it will fade away in the distance.
The moment it fades away into the far distance
you have discovered something:
there is no interference.
The mind is no longer poking its nose in,
and suddenly you become aware
of your own intrinsic nature
and with that is the beginning of miracles.

raised this most ordinary thing into the most extraordinary. They have bridged "this" and "that" — as if tea and God have become one.

Unless tea becomes divine you will not be divine, because the least has to be raised to the greatest, the ordinary has to be raised to the extraordinary, the earth has to be made heaven. They have to be bridged, no gap should be left.

Zen says both the ordinary and the extraordinary, both the earth and heaven are real, but they are not two. Bridge them — so tea becomes prayer, so the most profane thing becomes the most sacred. It is a symbol. And Zen says if your ordinary life becomes extraordinary, only then are you spiritual. Otherwise, you are not spiritual. In the ordinary the extraordinary has to be found; in the familiar, the strange; in the known, the unknown; in the near, the far; in "this," "that."

So Joshu said, "Come and have a cup of tea."

One more dimension is there in the story, and that dimension is of welcome. Everybody is welcome. Who you are is not relevant, you are welcome. At the gate of an enlightened master, at the gate of a Joshu or a Buddha, everybody is welcome. The door is, in a sense, open: "Come in and have a cup of tea." What does this mean, "Come in and have a cup of tea"? Joshu was saying, "Come in and relax."

If you go to other so-called masters, so-called monks and renunciates, you will become more tense; you cannot relax. Go to a renunciate — you become more tense, you become more afraid. And he creates guilt; he will look at you with condemnatory eyes, and the very way he looks at you will say you are a sinner. And he will start condemning: "This is wrong, that is wrong; leave this, leave that."

This is not the way of a really enlightened person. He will make you feel relaxed. There is a Chinese saying that if you reach a really great man you will feel relaxed with him; if you reach a false great man he will create tension within you. He will make, knowingly or unknowingly, every effort to show that you are low, a sinner; that he is high, above, transcendental.

A buddha will help you to relax, because only in your deep relaxation will you also become a buddha. There is no other way.

"Have a cup of tea," Joshu said. "Come relax with me." The tea is symbolic — relax. If you are drinking tea with a buddha, you will immediately feel that you are not alien, not strangers. Buddha pouring tea in your cup... Buddha has come down to you. Buddha has come to "this," he has brought "that" to "this." Christians, Jews, cannot conceive it; Mohammedans cannot conceive it. If you knock at the gate of heaven, can you conceive of God coming and telling you, "Come, have a cup of tea"? It looks so profane! God will be sitting on his throne looking at you with his thousand eyes, looking at every nook and corner of your being, at how many sins you have committed. Judgment will be there.

This Joshu is nonjudgmental. He does not judge you, he

simply accepts. Whatsoever you say, he accepts and says, "Come and relax with me." Relaxation is the point. And if you can relax with an enlightened person, his enlightenment will start penetrating you because when you are relaxed you become porous. When you are tense you are closed; when you relax he will enter. When you are relaxed, comfortable, drinking tea, Joshu is doing something then. He cannot enter through your mind but he can enter through your heart. Asking you to have a cup of tea is making you relaxed, friendly, bringing you nearer, closer.

Remember, whenever you are taking food and drinking something with someone, you become very intimate. Food and sex are the only two intimacies. In sex you are intimate, in food you are intimate. And food is more basic an intimacy than sex, because when a child is born the first thing he will receive from the mother will be food. Sex will come later on, when he becomes mature sexually — fourteen, fifteen years later. The first thing you received in this world was food, and that food was a drink. So the first intimacy known in this world is between a mother and a child.

Joshu was saying, "Come, have a cup of tea. Let me become your mother. Let me give you a drink." And a master is a mother — I insist that a master is a mother. A master is not a father, and Christians are wrong when they call their priests "father" because the father is a very unnatural thing, a societal phenomenon. The father doesn't exist anywhere in nature except in human society; it is a created thing, a cultured thing. The mother is natural. It exists without any culture, education, society, it is there in nature. Even trees have mothers. You may not have heard that not only does your mother give you life, but even a tree has a mother. They have been experimenting in England. There is a special lab where they have been experimenting with plants, and they have come to discover a very mysterious phenomenon. If a seed is thrown in the soil, and the mother from where the seed has been taken is near, it sprouts sooner. If the mother is not near, it takes a longer time. If the mother has been destroyed, cut, then it takes a very long time for the seed to sprout. The presence of the mother, even for a seed, is helpful.

A master is a mother, he is not a father. With a father you are related only intellectually, with a mother your relation is total. You have been part of your mother, you belong to her totally. The same is the case with a master in the reverse order. You have come out of the mother, you will go into the master. It is a returning back to the source.

So Zen masters always invite you for a drink. They are saying in a symbolic way, "Come and become a child to me, let me become your mother; let me become your second womb. Enter me, I will give you a rebirth."

Food is intimacy, it is love. And Zen masters always invite you for tea. They will take you in the tearoom and give you tea; they are giving you food, drink. They are telling you, "Become intimate. Don't stand so far away come nearer. Feel at home."

These are the dimensions of the story, but they are dimensions of feeling. You cannot understand but you can feel, and feeling is a higher understanding; love is a higher knowing. And the heart is the supreme center of knowledge, not the mind. The mind is just secondary, workable, utilitarian. You can know the surface through the mind, you can never know the center.

The heart has its own ways of knowing. Joshu can be understood only through the heart.

Practice

FIND THE SACRED
IN THE ORDINARY

For the man of Zen everything is sacred, even taking a cup of tea. Whatever he does, he does as if he is in a holy space.

There is a story about Moses. When he went on Mount Sinai to meet God and to receive the Ten Commandments, he saw a miracle happening: a green bush, lush green, and inside it a beautiful flame. As he approached it, somebody shouted from the bush, "Take your shoes off! This is holy ground." The Judaic interpretation is that the flame was God himself. That's why the bush was not burning, because God's fire is cool. And Moses unconsciously was entering into the area, which was like a temple or a synagogue: the living God was there. He took his shoes off and went in.

I don't think there is anything historical in it, but there is one thing significant: that wherever God is, the ground becomes holy.

Zen approaches things from the very other extreme: wherever there is sacredness, God is. Wherever there is holiness, God is. Not vice versa — not that God's presence makes any place holy, but if you make any place holy, the presence of the divine, of godliness, is immediately felt there. So they have tried to bring the sacred into everything. No other religion has gone that far, that high, that deep.

No other religion has even conceived the idea.

In Zen there is no God. In Zen there is only you and your consciousness. Your consciousness is the highest flowering in existence up to now. It can go still higher, and the way to take it higher is to create your whole life in such a way that it becomes sacred.

A cup of tea is the most ordinary thing, but they make in every monastery a special temple for drinking tea, surrounded by beautiful trees, ponds... a small temple. You enter into the temple, taking your shoes off, and Zen believes, "Where you leave your shoes, leave yourself too." So you enter into the temple absolutely pure, uncontaminated.

In the tea house, the tea temple, nobody talks. Only silence deepens. Everybody sits in the Zen meditative posture. The samovar is preparing the hot water for the tea, and the sound of the samovar has to be listened to as carefully as you have listened to your master. It does not matter what you are listening to, what matters is how you are listening.

Zen changes everything and takes a far more significant posture: it is not a question of what you are listening to, it is a question of how you are listening. So it doesn't matter whether the master is speaking or the sound of the samovar. And everybody is sitting there silently while the tea is being prepared.

Listening to the samovar... slowly the aroma, the fragrance of the tea leaves fills the temple. You have to be available to it as if it is divine grace. It is transforming everything small — the smallest, most negligible things — into something very significant, meaningful... giving it a religious color. And then the woman who is tending the tea will come to you. Her grace in pouring tea into your cups, and the silence, and the sound of the samovar, and the fragrance of fresh tea, creates a magic of its own.

Nobody speaks. Everybody starts sipping the tea, tasting as totally as possible, being in the moment as intensely as possible, as if the whole world has disappeared. Only the tea is there, you are there — and the silence.

Now, a very mundane affair... all over the world people drink tea and coffee and everything, but nobody has been able to transform the character of the mundane into the sacred.

As the tea is finished, they bow down to the woman with respect. Slowly they go out of the temple without making any noise. In fact people all over the world don't enter into temples with such silence; in the temple all kinds of talking and gossips are going on. Women are inquiring about each other's jewelry and clothes — in fact they go there to show off their jewelry and clothes; they don't have any other place to exhibit their possessions. All the temples and churches are nothing but gossiping clubs where people go to gossip about all kinds of mundane things. They destroy the whole meaning.

And Zen has changed a very ordinary thing into an extraordinary experience. You will never forget drinking tea with a man of Zen. You will be fortunate if the master is present. Every gesture is filled with significance.

It is called a tea ceremony, not tea drinking. It is not a teashop or a cafe, it is a temple. Here, ceremonies happen. This is only symbolic. In the whole of life, around the clock, you have to remember that wherever you are it is a holy land and whatever you are doing it is divine.

But just remembering will not be of much help. It is supported by meditation; otherwise it will remain a mind thing, it won't go deep. That meditation is always there to give it depth. So the whole day in a Zen monastery, from the morning when people get up till the night when they go to sleep, is a long prayer. They are not praying — there is no God to pray to — but they are prayerful, they are thankful, they are grateful. And with the meditation in the background, each small thing starts having new significances that you had never thought about.

Who had thought that a cup of tea could have some spiritual significance? But in Zen it has. If you look just on the surface it may look like a ritual. If you are an outsider, it may look like a ritual. You have to be an insider to understand that it is not a ritual; they are really living it, enjoying it, because behind it is the world of meditation, silence.

It is not only the silence in the temple; a greater silence is within them. It is not only the holiness outside; a greater holiness is within them. The whole day they are whole — whatever they are doing: cleaning the grounds of the monastery, working in the garden, cutting wood, carrying water from the well, cooking food. Whatever they are doing, they are doing so totally that unless you are an insider you can see only their action. You will not be able to see from where that action arises — the oceanic depth within them.

It happened: One emperor of Japan went to see Nan-In, a famous Zen master and one of the strangest masters of all. The emperor had heard much about him. Many times he had invited Nan-In to come to the court, to be a guest of the emperor, but he always received the message, "It is always the thirsty that goes to the well, not the well to the thirsty."

Finally, the emperor decided to go himself. When he went inside the gate of the monastery... it was on a mountain, surrounded with thick jungle, and one man was chopping wood. That was the first man he met. The emperor asked him, "Where is the master? Can I see him?"

The man stopped and said, "Yes, you can see him. Just go directly ahead and you will reach the place where he lives." And he started chopping wood again.

And as the emperor was going on he shouted, "Don't disturb the place. Just sit down and wait. The master comes whenever he feels like coming. That is his mastery."

The emperor thought, "Strange people. Just a woodcutter, but he talks with the emperor in such a manner that if he were in the court he would have been beheaded! But here it is better to be silent and go."

So he went and sat at the cottage where the master was supposed to come. After a few minutes, the master came. And the emperor was puzzled, because he was dressed in the robe of the master but his face looked exactly like the woodcutter.

Looking at his puzzled face, the master said, "Don't be worried, we have met before. I was chopping wood; I had directed you to this place."

The emperor said, "But why did you not say then and there that you are the master?"

He said, "At that time I was not. I was just a wood-chopper, a woodcutter — so totally involved in it that I had absolutely no place left for the master. That's why I told you to wait, so that I could finish with my wood, take a shower, put on the master's robe, remember that now I am a master, and be total in it. Now I am ready. For what have you come?"

The emperor said, "I have completely forgotten for what I had come! Seeing the situation, that the master chops wood — don't you have disciples? I have heard that you have five hundred disciples."

He said, "Yes, I have. They are in the monastery, deeper in the forest. But chopping wood is such a joy that I would rather chop wood than be a master. It is such a sacred, such a blissful feeling, the cool breeze, the hot sun, the whole body perspiring, and each hit of the axe making the silence of the place deeper. Next time you come, join me! We do all kinds of things that are necessary, but one thing remains common as a golden thread running through all actions, and that is meditation. And meditation makes everything divine. Then actions don't count. What counts is your consciousness at the moment of the action."

This is changing the whole ideology of ordinary mind. Ordinary mind judges the act, it never bothers about the consciousness out of which the action is born.

An action coming out of meditation becomes sacred, and the same action without meditation is mundane.

We have made our lives full of mundane things, mundane acts, because we don't know a simple secret that can transform the quality of everything that we do. And remember, if you don't know the secret of transformation, amongst those mundane things you are also mundane. Unless you have a consciousness, which makes you sacred and holy, which is going to transform everything that you do into the same category in which you *are*...

Whatever you will touch will become sacred.

Whatever you will do will become holy.

Zen is the very essence of all religions, without their stupid rituals, nonsensical theologies. It has dropped everything that could be dropped. It has saved only that which is the very soul of religiousness.

SLOW DOWN

Life is not going anywhere; there is no goal to it, no destination. Life is non-purposive, it simply is. Unless this understanding penetrates your heart, you cannot slow down.

Slowing down is not a question of any "how;" it is not a question of technique, method. We reduce everything into a how. There is a great how-to-ism all over the world, and every person, particularly the modern, contemporary mind, has become a how-to-er. How to do this, how to do that, how to grow rich, how to be successful, how to influence people and win friends, how to meditate, even how to love. The day is not far off when some stupid guy is going to ask how to breathe.

It is not a question of how at all. Don't reduce life to technology. Life reduced to technology loses all flavor of joy.

I have come across a book; the name of the book is hilarious. The name is, *You Must Relax*. Now the "must" is the problem! But it is there. It is because of the *must* that nobody is able to relax. Now this *must* on top of all other musts — *You Must Relax* — is going to create more tension in your life. Try to relax, and you will find out that you feel more tense than ever. Try harder and you will feel more tense and more tense.

Relaxation is not a consequence, is not a result of some activity; it is the glow of understanding.

This is the first thing I would like to relate to you: life is purposeless. It is very hard to accept it. And why is it so hard to accept that life is purposeless? It is hard because without purpose the ego cannot exist. It is hard to conceive that life has no goal, because without any goal there is no point in having a mind, in having an ego.

The ego can exist only in a goal-oriented vision; the mind can exist only in the future. The purpose brings future in; the goal creates the space for thoughts to move, desires to arise. And then naturally there is hurry, because life is short. Today we are here and tomorrow we are gone — maybe even the next moment. Life is very short.

If there is a goal to be achieved, there is bound to be hurry. And there is bound to be worry, a constant worry: "Am I going to make it or not?" — a trembling heart, a shaking of the foundations. You will remain almost always in an inner earthquake, you will be always on the verge of a nervous breakdown. Have a goal, and sooner or later you will end up on the psychoanalyst's couch.

My vision is that of a goalless life. That is the vision of all the buddhas. Everything simply is, for no reason at all. Everything simply is utterly absurd. If this is understood, then where is the hurry, and for what? Then you start living moment to moment. Then this moment is given to you, a gracious gift from God, or the whole, or whatsoever you want to call it — Tao, dhamma, logos.

This moment is available to you — sing a song, live it in its totality. And don't try to sacrifice it for any other

People are in a hurry. I have come to know people who have meditated three days, and on the fourth day they ask, "Three days we have been meditating, why has nothing happened yet? As if they are obliging existence by meditating for so long—three days, one hour every day; that means three hours! And if you actually look, in their meditation they were just daydreaming; with closed eyes they were daydreaming. They call it meditation! And just because for three days they have been sitting for one hour, with great difficulty, somehow managing—great noise inside, no silence, no peace, no consciousness, just desires, thoughts, memories, imagination, constant traffic, a crowd—then they come on the fourth day, saying, "What is happening? Three days have passed and nothing has happened yet."

Time should not be taken into account at all—three years, not even three lives. You should not think in terms of time, because the phenomenon of meditation is nontemporal. It can happen any moment, it can happen right now. It may take years, it may take lives. It all depends on your intensity, on your sincerity, and it all depends on your totality.

moment that is going to come in the future. Live it for its own sake.

They say art is for art's sake. It may be so, it may not be so; I am not an artist. But I can say to you: Life is for life's sake. Each moment is utterly for its own sake.

Live in the moment for the sheer joy of living it. Don't have any ideals, don't try to make something out of yourself, don't try to improve upon God. You are perfect as you are. With all your imperfections you are perfect. If you are imperfect, you are perfectly imperfect — but perfection is there.

Once this is understood, where is the hurry? Where is the worry? You have already slowed down. And then it is a morning walk with no destination, going nowhere. You can enjoy each tree and each sunray and each bird and each person that passes by.

Meditations and Ceremonies

The tea ceremony is only the beginning. I say unto you:
Your every act should be a ceremony.
If you can bring your consciousness, your awareness,
your intelligence to the act, if you can be spontaneous,
then there is no need for any other religion.
Life itself will be the religion.

1. CUP-EMPTYING

Somebody has sent me a beautiful anecdote.

Pat O'Reilly was confessing his sins. "Sure, Father, I had sex seven times last night."

The priest asked, "How many women?"

"Ah, Father, there was only one woman," answered Pat.

To which the priest said, "Well, it is not as bad as I thought. Who is the woman?"

"My wife, Father."

"Well," said the priest, "there is nothing wrong with that, son."

"I know, Father," replied Pat, "but I just had to tell someone!"

There are moments when you just have to tell someone. If you don't tell, it becomes heavy on you. If you tell, you are released and relaxed. If you can find a sympathetic listener, good; otherwise just talk to yourself. But don't repress it. Repressed, it will become a burden on you. Just sit in front of the wall and have a good talk. In the beginning you will feel it is a little crazy, but the more you do it, the more you will see the beauty of it. It is not violent. It does not waste somebody else's time, and it works the same way, it does the same: you are relieved. And after a good talk with the wall you will feel very, very relaxed. In fact, everybody needs to do it. The world would be better and more silent if people started talking to the walls.

Try it. It will be deep meditation — knowing well that the wall is not listening. But that is not the point.

I have heard about a great psychoanalyst who became very old but still continued to practice six, seven, eight hours per day, listening to the patients. He had a young disciple, an apprentice, who became tired after three or four hours — listening to nonsense, neurotic obsessions, fixations, the same thing again and again. He asked his old master one day, "How do you manage? Because I see you as fresh in the evening as in the morning when you come to the clinic. You are as fresh as when you go — seven, eight hours of nonsense. You never get tired. I get tired after two, three hours — and I am a young man!"

The old man laughed and said, "Who listens?"

Freud arranged it very well. He did not even face the patient. He would tell the patient to lie on a couch, and there would be a curtain, and behind the curtain he would sit. And the patient lying on the couch, looking at the ceiling, had to talk. It was really very meaningful. First, when a person is lying down he is more relaxed. He talks of deeper things than when he is sitting. He goes deeper

into his unconscious. Talk to a man standing, and he will be very superficial. Sit down, and he goes a little deeper. Let him lie down and then listen to him; he goes very deep.

And then, he is not facing anybody. When you are facing somebody the very presence of the other functions as a repressive force. Then you start saying things that you know he will like. Then you start saying things in such a way that he is not offended. Then you manage somehow to say things that will be approved by him. Then there is much repression; then the truth never comes out. When the man is not facing you, and you are just facing the ceiling, you have nothing to manage. The ceiling will never be offended, you can say anything you like. By and by, one goes deep into associations.

There is no need for the Freudian couch, simply your bedroom will do. And there is no need for anybody to sit there, you can just talk and listen to yourself. Talking and listening to yourself will give you a depth, a great understanding about your own mind.

So talk to the wall, and listen. Be both the talker and the listener. Don't analyze, don't judge, don't say "this is good and that is bad...that should not be said and this should be said," no. And don't make any refinement, don't polish it. Simply blurt out whatsoever comes to the mind — ugly, absurd, irrelevant. Let the mind have full play and you simply watch. It will be a very great meditation.

The new groom was singing the praises of married life to
his bachelor friend. "Yes, it is wonderful. Breakfast before
I go to work is large and delicious. When I go off after that,
the little woman gives me a big hug and kiss at the door.
I return home at night, supper is on the table. After that
I sit in the living room reading the paper while the missus
cleans away the dishes. Then she changes into something
more comfortable and sits down beside me, and talks to me.
And she talks, and talks, and talks, until I wish she would
drop dead."

Don't give such an opportunity to anybody that he starts
thinking, "When are you going to drop dead?" It is your
problem. Or, you can make a good arrangement if somebody else has the same problem. There are so many mad
people; you can find somebody else who has the same
problem. Then you can make an arrangement: one hour
you talk, one hour you listen to the other person. No need
to be connected with each other, no need to be relevant,
and no need to follow any rules of conversation. It is not
a conversation. One hour you blurt out whatsoever comes
to your mind, and of course, then you have to pay — one
hour you have to listen. And it will be valuable for both.

But one thing should be remembered: don't repress it.
Anything repressed becomes poisonous. And talking is just
innocent; the wall will do. Go to the trees and they will feel
very happy; nobody talks to them. They are always waiting.
They will feel grateful. Or go to the river or to the rocks,

but don't repress. By and by, things will clear up and talking will disappear. It is just the beginning. Then deeper layers of being will be touched. Talk is the most superficial layer of your life, just a very superficial layer. When energy is flowing deep, that layer starts trembling, ripples arise. Allow them. Soon, when the talk is exhausted and you have thrown out all the rubbish that you have been carrying for your whole life, silence will come. And that silence will be completely uncorrupted, virgin. You can force your talking underground, you can repress it and you can look silent, but your silence will not be real silence. Deep down the tremor will continue; deep down the volcano is getting ready to erupt any moment. You are sitting on top of it.

People look silent but they are not silent. I would like you to become really silent, and the way is a deep catharsis.

And a good talker has something valuable: he can communicate better. To be articulate is beautiful because communication is more possible. And a good talk is an aesthetic value in itself. But first, let the flood be thrown out. Then things will sort themselves out, then things will settle. But first this flood has to go.

All the great scriptures of the world are written in sutras, aphorisms — because the people who wrote them went through this flood of catharsis. When the catharsis was complete, then diamond-like, small sentences — simple, aesthetic, beautiful, complete — started bubbling in the consciousness. It is from that consciousness that the Vedas were born, and the Koran. And it is from that consciousness

THE ULTIMATE IS NOT SOMEWHERE FAR AWAY.

The ultimate is very close by.

In the very immediate it is present,

in the very immediate it is pulsating.

The immediate is the heartbeat of the ultimate

that the beauty of the language of the Bible arises. Never again has it been surpassed.

Jesus was illiterate, but nobody has ever surpassed that clarity, that penetrating reality of his assertions. Behind it is great meditation. The *Yoga Sutras* of Patanjali or the *Brahma Sutras* of Badrayana or the *Bhakti Sutras* of Narad — small sentences, the smallest you can conceive, almost telegraphic — but so much is pressed into them that each sentence has atomic energy. If you lovingly take it into yourself, to your heart, it will explode and you will become luminous through it.

But first the flood has to go. Allow it. If you can find some sympathetic ears, good. Otherwise, trees, rocks, but don't repress it.

2. BE PRESENT TO THE PRESENT

The mind disappears whenever you stop planning for the future. The mind is nothing but a projection of the future. It disappears when you start living moment to moment.

Live moment to moment. For three weeks, try. Whatsoever you are doing, do it as totally as possible. Love it and enjoy it. Maybe it looks silly. If you are drinking tea it is silly to enjoy it too much — it is just ordinary tea.

But ordinary tea can become extraordinarily beautiful — a tremendous experience if you enjoy it. Enjoy it with deep reverence. Make it a ceremony. Making tea... Listening to the kettle and the sound. Then pouring the tea... smelling the fragrance of it. Then tasting the tea and feeling happy.

Dead people cannot drink tea, only very alive people. This moment you are alive! This moment you are drinking tea. Feel thankful! And don't think of the future. Next moment will take care of itself. Think not of the morrow. For three weeks live in the moment and see what happens.

3. BRING YOURSELF BACK TO THE NOW

We are very unalert. We think much of the past and we also think much of the future and our whole life is wasted in that thinking. Because between these two — the past and the future — the present is crushed, sandwiched, and has almost become negligible, it has become so small. The real has become small and the unreal has grown so big.

If you think of the past, it is long: your past, then the society's past, then humanity's past, then the past of life on earth and then the earth's past, and then the sun and the moon and the stars; it is infinite. And so is the future infinite: it will go on and on. Compared to the past and future, the present seems almost nothing — it is just a small point, atomic — and between these two it is almost lost. And the present is the only reality; everything else is unreal compared to it.

If you see a rose flower you see it now, in the now. If you smell it, you smell it in the now. If you feel and touch it, you touch it in the now. You cannot touch the rose flower in the future and you cannot smell the rose flower in the past. But if you start thinking of past and future, then the rose flower is there and yet is not there; it disappears.

ONCE AWARENESS IS BORN, *slowly slowly you are getting out of the past and out of the future and you are entering the present. You are becoming more present to the present. You are attaining to a kind of presence which was never there; you are becoming luminous. And in this presence, when you can feel the moment passing by, all your senses will become so pure, so sensitive, so sensuous, so alert and alive, that the whole life will take a new intensity. You will attain to a great zestfulness. The world will be the same, and yet not the same: the trees will look greener, the roses rosier, the people more alive, more beautiful—the same world, and the pebbles on the shore start looking like diamonds and emeralds.*

When awareness is very, very deep-rooted, when you are present to the present, you attain to a psychedelic vision of life.

Just meditate on this: you are facing a rose flower, a beautiful rose flower. It is there — the fragrance is released into your nostrils, you are delighted with it. Now bring the past in. Think of something in the past: somebody insulted you yesterday or yesteryear. Or think of a childhood incident, your mother was beating you. Bring it into memory and suddenly the mind is clouded. Now you will not feel the presence of the flower so much. It is still there, the same flower, but you are no longer here; you are distracted, you have become foggy, clouded. A screen of memory has come between you and the rose flower.

Or think of the future — some plan, some fantasy, something that you want to do tomorrow — and the flower fades, bows out further and further. The deeper in thought you go, the farther the flower recedes. Come out of the thought and the sky is clear, the clouds have separated and again the sunshine and again the presence of the flower; you can again smell it. While you were thinking of the past and the future the smell was still knocking at the doors of your nose, but you were not available. The color of the flower was still coming to your eyes but you were not there. It was as if you were looking through a dark glass; things became unclear, hazy, a mist surrounded you.

The whole work of meditation is nothing but this: how to become utterly present in the present, how to collect oneself in the now. Then everything is beautiful. Then walking is meditation, sitting is meditation, talking is meditation, listening is meditation, because whether you

WHEN YOU TOUCH, BECOME THE TOUCH.

When you see, become the eyes.

When you hear, your whole consciousness

must come to the ears.

Listening to a song, or listening to the birds,

become the ears.

Forget everything else so it is as if you are only the ears.

Come to the ears with your total being.

Then, your ears will become more sensitive.

When you are looking at something — a flower

or a beautiful face or the stars — become the eyes.

Forget everything else,

as if the whole rest of your body

has gone out of existence

and your consciousness has become just eyes.

Then your eyes will be able to look more deeply,

and you will become capable

of looking at the invisible also.

The invisible can also be seen,

but you need more penetrating eyes to see it.

walk or sit, it is always now; whether you are silent or talking it is always now. There is only one time. Now is eternity.

Let this be the key. You have to work on it, you have to play around this idea more and more. In whatsoever you are doing, again and again pull yourself into the present. In the beginning the mind rebels, resists; old patterns are powerful, old habits go on dragging you here and there. But slowly, slowly as the joy of the present deepens, as you start becoming more and more saturated with it, as you see the contentment that arises out of it and the silence and the celebration, the old patterns are broken, the habits disappear.

4. SWITCH ON YOUR SENSES

Each child is born with beautiful senses. Watch a child. When he looks at something, he is completely absorbed. When he is playing with his toys, he is utterly absorbed. When he looks, he becomes just the eyes. Look at the eyes of a child. When he hears, he becomes just the ears. When he eats something, he is just there on the tongue. He becomes just the taste. See a child eating an apple. With what gusto! With what great energy! With what delight! See a child running after a butterfly in the garden... so absorbed that even if God were available, he would not run that way. Such a tremendous, meditative state — and without any effort. See a child collecting seashells on the beach as if he were collecting diamonds. Everything is

precious when the senses are alive. Everything is clear
when the senses are alive.

Later on in life, the same child will look at reality as if
hidden behind a darkened glass. Much smoke and dust have
gathered on the glass, and you are hidden behind it and
you are looking. Because of this, everything looks dull and
dead. You look at the tree and the tree looks dull because
your eyes are dull. You hear a song, but there is no appeal
in it because your ears are dull.

Reclaim your forgotten language. Whenever you have
time, be more in your senses. Eating — don't just eat, try
to learn the forgotten language of taste again. Touch the
bread, feel the texture of it. Feel with open eyes, feel with
closed eyes. While chewing, chew it — you are chewing
God. Remember it! It will be disrespectful not to chew
well, not to taste well. Let it be a prayer, and you will start
the rising of a new consciousness in you.

Touch people more. We have become very touchy about
touch. If somebody is talking to you and comes too close,
you start moving backwards. We protect our territory.
We don't touch and we don't allow others to touch; we
don't hold hands, we don't hug. We don't enjoy each
other's being.

Go to the tree, touch the tree. Touch the rock. Go to
the river, let the river flow through your hands. Feel it!
Swim, and feel the water again as the fish feels it. Don't
miss any opportunity to revive your senses. And there are
a thousand and one opportunities the whole day. There is

no need to have some separate time for it. The whole day is a training in sensitivity. Use all the opportunities. Sitting under your shower, use the opportunity — feel the touch of the water falling on you. Lie down on the ground, naked, feel the earth. Lie down on the beach, feel the sand. Listen to the sounds of the sand, listen to the sounds of the sea. Use every opportunity — only then will you be able to learn the language of the senses again.

5. **LEARN TO LISTEN**

You listen, everyone listens, but right listening is a rare achievement. So what is the difference between listening and right listening?

Right listening means not just a fragmentary listening. I am saying something, you are listening to it. Your ears are being used; you may not be just behind your ears at all; you may have gone somewhere else. You may not be present. If you are not present in your totality, then it cannot be right listening.

Right listening means you have becomes just your ears — the whole being is listening. No thinking inside, no thoughts, no thought process, only listening. Try it sometimes; it is a deep meditation in itself. Some birds are singing — the crows — just become listening, forget everything — just be the ears. The wind is passing through the trees, the leaves are rustling; just become the ears, forget everything — no thought process, just listen. Become the ears. Then it is right listening, then your whole

In a small school it happened
that a small boy sitting in the
rear of the classroom appeared
to be daydreaming.

"Johnny," asked the teacher,
"do you have trouble hearing?"

"No ma'am," he replied,
"I have trouble listening."

Listening is totally different
from hearing. Listening means
hearing without mind; listening
means hearing without any
interference of your thoughts;
listening means hearing as if
you are totally empty. If you
have even a small trembling
of thinking inside, waves of
subtle thoughts surrounding you,
you will not be able to listen,
although you will be able to hear.
And to listen to the music, the
ancient music, the eternal music,
one needs to be totally quiet —
as if one is not.

When you are, you can hear;
when you are not, you can listen.

being is absorbed into it, then you are totally present.

And the Hindu Upanishads say that the esoteric, ultimate formulas of spiritual alchemy cannot be given to you unless you are in a moment of right listening. These spiritual formulas — ultimate, secret keys — cannot be handed over to you as you are: unconscious of yourself, fragmentary, partial, listening but not present. These keys can be handed to you only when your total being has become receptive to take them in. They are seeds, and the seeds are powerful; they will explode in you. And they will begin to grow in you, but one has to become just a womb to receive them. If your ears have become just wombs to receive, and your total presence is there; if your whole body is listening — every fiber, every cell of the body is listening — only then these "great sentences" as they are called, *mahavakyas*, can be delivered to you.

So it has been a tradition in India, in the old India of ancient days, not to write down these *mahavakyas*, these great secret formulas — because if they are written, anyone can read them. He may not be ready. He may not be reading, he may not be listening, but he can become acquainted and that acquaintance becomes a barrier. He can begin to feel that he knows — but these secrets are not to be known through words, they can be known only through experience.

So the *rishis*, the writers of these Upanishads insisted for centuries not to write at all. These secrets were given from one individual to another, and not in an ordinary way

— in a very extraordinary process. A teacher, a master would give these secrets to a disciple. And the disciple must wait, sometimes for years; just being near the master, forgetting himself completely; just becoming attention, just being attentive — constantly remaining in the presence of the master and waiting for the right moment. And the disciple cannot decide when the right moment is, so leaving it to the master, remaining in a let-go and waiting... and suddenly one day, any moment, the master will say it. When the master finds that now you can listen with your total being, that now you have become a womb, just receptivity, and now the secrets can be handed to you — then he will tell you.

When the mind is utterly silent you are capable of listening. Then you are capable of listening to the song of the birds, a distant call of the cuckoo. Then you are able to listen even to the silence. Just now, listen to the silence... not only sound but soundlessness can be listened to. But you have to be noiseless.

Sometimes just become aware of your ears, as if you are just the ears and nothing else, as if your whole body has become the ears. Just be ears, and you will be surprised that you become aware of such subtle noises, such subtle happenings around you that you have never been aware of. You may start hearing your own breathing, your own heartbeat. You may start hearing many things — and you have lived always amongst these things, but you were never

Silence is not a word

it is an experience.

It is not a doctrine, a dogma

but a taste on the tongue.

Something to be eaten, to be drunk, to be digested

something that becomes part

of your blood, bones and very marrow.

aware; you were so occupied into yourself.

In Zen they have a koan: to listen to the sound of one hand clapping. They call this the deepest meditation: to try to listen to some sound that is uncreated. If you go on meditating, go on meditating — just sitting and meditating, trying to listen — you will hear many things. This is one of the most beautiful techniques. Just close your eyes, sit under a tree and start listening. You will hear many new sounds that you were never aware of before. Birds, insects… Slowly, very slowly, you will become aware of many sounds around you. Go on finding out which sound is uncreated.

Every sound will be created. One bird starts singing and then it stops. That which was created has now moved into nonexistence. Go on listening, go on listening. Go on trying to find out which is the sound that is uncreated. By and by, more subtle sounds will be heard. You will start hearing your own heartbeats, you will start hearing your own breathing. But that too is created. Your heart will stop, your breathing cannot continue forever. It was not always there. When a child is born there is no breathing. Then suddenly the child starts crying and breathing starts.

Go on listening deeply. These are not soundless sounds. Throw them, eliminate them. You will start listening to the sound of your blood circulating. More subtle. You are not ordinarily aware of your blood circulating. You will hear it circulating, you will hear the sound. But it is also a created sound, created through circulation, through conflict. Go on eliminating. If you persist long enough, finally a moment

will come when all sounds have disappeared; you cannot hear anything. A gap is created; all sounds have disappeared. And with these sounds, the whole universe has disappeared for you, as if you have fallen into an emptiness.

Don't be afraid now. Otherwise you will fall back again to the world of sounds. Remain unafraid. It will look like a death. It is, because when all sounds have been lost, you have lost your mind also. Your mind is just a chattering box. You no longer have a mind. With no more sounds, the world is no longer there. You will feel as if you have died; you are no more. You were nothing but a combination, a collection, of sounds.

Persist. This death is beautiful because it is the door to the divine. Go on trying to listen to what is now there. After the gap, if you have traveled it without becoming afraid and scared....

If you are scared, you will fall back again; you will again run back to the world of sounds. The mind will start functioning again. But if you are unafraid and can persist in this gap of soundlessness, you will become aware of a new sound that is uncreated. This sound Hindus have called *omkar*: AUM. AUM is just a symbol for the sound that is always there in the innermost core. AUM, AUM, AUM — this is going on inside, uncreated. No one is uttering it. It is just there.

This is the soundless sound, uncreated.

6. ACCEPT EVERYTHING

Distraction is not something objective, not there outside you; it is something in you. If you cannot accept, you will be distracted; if you accept, distraction disappears.

Once it happened: I was staying in a rest house. And a political leader was also staying there — a very small rest house in a very small village. The political leader came to me in the middle of the night, and said, "It is impossible to sleep. How are you sleeping?" He shook me, and said, "How are you sleeping, there is so much distraction?"

Somehow or other at least two dozen dogs... they must have made the rest house their abode — the whole village's dogs. Maybe they were having a political gathering also — and they were so many; there was such a loud barking and fighting.

He said, "But how are you sleeping? These dogs won't allow me to sleep, and I am tired."

So I said to the political leader, "But they are not aware of you. They don't read newspapers, they don't listen to the radio, they don't look at television; they are not aware of you. I was also here before you. That is their usual way: they are not doing it specially for you. You are fighting, resisting. The notion that they are disturbing you is disturbing you; not they. Accept them." I told him to do one small meditation. "Lie down on the bed. Enjoy their barking. Let it be a music. Enjoy it. Listen to it, as attentively as possible."

He said, "How is it going to help me? I want to avoid,

I want to forget that they are there, and you are telling me to listen to them. That will disturb me even more."

I told him, "You just try. You have been trying your way, and it has failed. Now try my way; and you can see that it has been successful with me."

He was not ready for it, and he didn't believe it; but there was no other way, so he tried. And within five minutes he was fast asleep, and snoring. So I went and shook him up, and I said, "How are you sleeping? How is it possible?"

If you accept, nothing can distract you. It is the very rejection in you that creates the distraction. So, if you want to meditate without distraction, don't reject anything. The traffic noise has to be accepted — it is part of this world, and perfectly okay; the child crying and weeping is part of this world, and perfectly okay. Once you say that everything is okay, just watch the feeling that everything is okay and accept it. Something within you melts. Then nothing distracts you.

7. TASTE

Bring your awareness to taste. When you are eating, forget everything else; just become your tongue, just your taste buds. Exist there in your totality. Taste your food as deeply as possible, and you will be in for a great surprise — not one but many surprises.

First you will become aware that you cannot eat more than is needed. You need not diet — only foolish people diet. And you can diet for a few days, and then you jump upon the food with a vengeance, and you gain more weight than you have lost! If you are intelligent, bring your awareness to your taste. Why do you eat more? The simple reason is that you don't taste, and your hunger for taste remains, so you go on stuffing more. If you really taste, soon you will be satisfied, contented. Soon the body will say, "Stop!" And if you are alert you will be able to listen when the body says stop.

Right now you are not there at all. You are eating, but you are not there, present. You may be in your office or you may have gone somewhere else, doing a thousand and one things. One thing is certain: that you are not at the table where you are sitting, you are always somewhere else. You are never where you are; you can't be found where you are.

Eat, but eat meditatively, silently. When you are eating you are talking. Don't talk, because if you are talking you will miss the joy of eating, and when you miss the joy of eating, your hunger for taste goes on asking for more, so you go on stuffing. And that seems to be nonending. People are stuffing the whole day and still it seems they are not satisfied. Eating twice may be enough or at the most thrice, but people are eating the whole day — particularly Americans! If they are not eating they won't know what else to do. Just doing something with the mouth keeps them occupied. If they are not eating they are talking, if they are not talking they are smoking, if they are not

ANOTHER STORY:

> Zen student: "So, master, is the soul immortal or
> not? Do we survive our bodily death or do we get
> annihilated? Do we really reincarnate? Does our soul
> split up into component parts, which get recycled, or
> do we as a single unit enter the body of a biological
> organism? And do we retain our memories or not?
> Or is the doctrine of reincarnation false? Is perhaps
> the Christian notion of survival more correct? And
> if so, do we get bodily resurrected, or does our soul
> enter a purely Platonic spiritual realm?"

> Master: "Your breakfast is getting cold."

That's the way of Zen: to bring you herenow. The
breakfast is far more important than any paradise.
The breakfast is far more important than any
concept of God. The breakfast is more important than
any theory of reincarnation, soul, rebirth, and all
that nonsense. Because the breakfast is herenow.

For Zen, the immediate is the ultimate, and the
imminent is the transcendental.

This moment is eternity... you have to be awakened
to this moment.

smoking they are chewing gum — as if the mouth has to remain continuously occupied.

Even when you are eating you are talking. How can you taste food and how can you be sensitive to taste?

When you go into the garden you are talking. If you are not talking with somebody else you are in a constant dialogue within yourself. You divide yourself into many persons, you make a crowd inside yourself. You are questioning and answering within yourself. You don't look at the flowers. You don't feel the fragrance, the joy of the birds, the celebration of the trees. You don't allow yourself any sensitivity, any opportunity to be more sensitive, to be more available to existence, to be more vulnerable.

Sensitivity means openness, vulnerability, availability.

People are either talking or reading newspapers or listening to the radio or watching the television — even five hours, six hours per day, watching television, destroying your eyes! And there is so much to see, and you are sitting before a box, glued to your chair!

Whatsoever you are doing... small things — eating, walking, drinking water, taking a bath, swimming in a river — whatsoever you are doing — lying down in the sun — be utterly there, be totally there.

Become your senses. Come down from the mind to the senses, come back to the senses.

8. BRING AWARENESS TO SMALL ACTS

Start becoming more and more conscious of everything that you are doing. Walking, walk consciously; bring your total attention to walking. And there is a great difference between when you just walk without any consciousness and when you bring the quality of consciousness to walking. The change is radical. It may not be visible from the outside, but from the inside it is really moving into another dimension.

Try some small act: for example, moving your hand. You can move it mechanically — then move it with great consciousness, feeling the movement, slowly, slowly, looking from the inside at how you are moving it. Just in this small gesture you are on the threshold of a great discovery, because a miracle is happening. It is one of the greatest mysteries, which science has not yet been able to fathom.

You decide that you should move the hand and the hand follows your decision. It is a miracle because it is consciousness contacting matter... not only that, but matter following consciousness. The bridge has not yet been found. It is magic! It is the power of mind over matter; that's what magic is all about. You do it the whole day, but you have not done it consciously; otherwise in this simple gesture a great meditation will arise in you. In this small gesture is the whole history of existence.

The scriptures say that God said, "Let there be light" and there was light. Now, it looks like utter nonsense if you think about it logically. How can there be light just by

saying "Let there be light"? But this is happening every day, all the time. When you say, "Let there be a movement in my hand" and the hand moves, it is the same miracle. And if you can feel it from the inside, awareness grows.

9. FIND THE BUDDHA WITHIN

Whenever you can find time — and at least once a day you have to find time.... Any time will do, but it is good to do it when the stomach is empty; more energy is available when the stomach is empty. Not that one should be hungry, just that the stomach should not be too full; if you have eaten then after two or three hours. Just a cup of tea is good... a cup of tea is very helpful. It makes you a little alert, so you can take a cup of tea but not anything else. Whenever you do it, early in the morning or in the night, the stomach should be empty.

The second thing: if you can take a bath before it that will be very helpful. Take a hot bath and a cold shower. First soak yourself in the hot bathtub and then just take a two-minute cold shower—but end with a cold shower; that will prepare you perfectly.

Then take a cup of tea and sit; make yourself comfortable. If you can sit on the floor, you can have a pillow underneath you, that will be good. If it feels difficult, or the posture is difficult, you can sit on a chair.

Relax the whole body and just concentrate on the middle of your chest, just in the middle where the rib bones and the stomach starts. With closed eyes, imagine that a small

Buddha statue is there, just an outline of a Buddha statue. You can have a picture of a small Buddha statue nearby so that you can visualize it better. Just a two-inch Buddha statue....

Visualize it as being made of light, and that rays are spreading out from it. Get absorbed in it, and it will work so that you can go into it easily... rays spreading, filling your whole body. If you can also sit in a Buddha posture on the floor that will be very helpful, because that figure and your posture will fit together. The rays are spreading and the whole body becomes full of light. Then the rays start spreading outside the body — just a visualization inside. The rays start touching the roof, the walls, and soon they are going outside the room; they go on spreading and they go on spreading.

Within fifteen minutes time let them cover the whole universe as far as you can conceive, and great peace will arise! Then remain in that state for at least for five to ten minutes: the whole universe full of rays and the center of that is in your innermost heart.

Hold that state for ten minutes, go on contemplating it, go on feeling the rays; go on and on and on. The whole universe is full of those rays. Then start shrinking back, slowly; as slowly as you had gone before, slowly shrink back. Then come back to your inner Buddha — again the two inch statue full of light.

Then suddenly let it disappear — abruptly; that is the point, the most significant point in the whole process.

Abruptly let it disappear and there will be left a negative image. It is just as when you look into a window too long and then you close your eyes and you see the negative image of the window.

The Buddha statue has been there, full of light; suddenly, abruptly, let it disappear. There will be a dark Buddha statue, a negative statue, emptiness... Hold that for at least five to ten minutes — that hole, that emptiness.

In the first stage when the rays are spreading all over the universe, you will feel great peace like you may have never felt before and a great expansion... a feeling that you have become huge and that the whole universe is in you.

In the second stage, instead of peace you will feel bliss-fulness. When the Buddha statue becomes negative and all light disappears and there is darkness and silence you will feel a great blissfulness... for no reason at all! A well-being arising in you — hold that.

So this whole process has to take not more than forty-five minutes, forty-five to sixty minutes. This will be very, very helpful.

And if you can sometimes do the Dynamic Meditation* also, both together will be of great importance, because the Dynamic is good for catharsis and this will be good for

---

* *Dynamic Meditation is an active meditation process developed by Osho especially for modern man, who often finds it difficult to sit silently without first releasing the accumulated tensions of mind and body. More information about the meditation can be found in Osho's book,* Meditation: The First and Last Freedom, *and on the* **osho.com** *website.*

silence. If you do the Dynamic in the morning, do this in the evening. If you cannot do two, then this one. And this one can be done in bed at night when you are going to sleep; that is the most perfect time. Do it and then just fall into sleep so the same state will continue vibrating the whole night.

Many times in your dreams that Buddha statue will appear, many times in your dreams those rays will be felt. In the morning you will feel that your sleep has been of a totally different quality. It was not just sleep: something more positive than sleep has been there, some presence has been there. You will come out more rejuvenated, more alert, more full of reverence for life.

10. BE TOTAL

Enjoy simple things with total intensity.

Just a cup of tea can be a deep meditation.

If you can enjoy it, the aroma of it, slowly sipping it, the taste of it... who cares about God?

You don't know that God is continuously feeling jealous of you when he sees you drinking a cup of tea and the poor fellow cannot have it. Instant coffee... these things are not available in the Garden of Eden.

And since Adam and Eve left, there is no human company at all — just living with animals, who don't know how to make tea.

God is very jealous of you and very repentant that he drove Adam and Eve out of the Garden of Eden, but now nothing

can be done about it. The sons and daughters of Adam and Eve are living far more beautifully, far more richly.

Enlightenment happens when you have forgotten all about it.

Don't look even out of the corner of your eye, just in case enlightenment is coming and you will miss it. Forget all about it. You just enjoy your simple life.

And everything is so beautiful — why create unnecessary anxiety and anguish for yourself? Strange problems of spirituality.... Those things are not something you can do anything about.

If you can make your ordinary life a thing of beauty and art, all that you had always desired will start happening of its own accord.

There is a beautiful story....

There is a temple in the state of Maharashtra, in India. It is a temple of Krishna, and a strange story is connected with the temple because the statue of Krishna — in Maharashtra he is called Bitthal — is standing on a brick. Strange, because nowhere in any temple is any god standing on a brick.

The story is that one beautiful man — enjoying life, every bit, in its totality — was so contented and so fulfilled that Krishna decided to appear before him. Ordinarily there are people who are singing and dancing their whole life, "Hare Krishna, Hare Rama" and neither Rama appears nor Krishna appears — nobody appears. And this man was not bothering about Krishna or Rama or anybody. He was

simply living his life, but living it the way it should be lived — with love, with heart, with beauty, with music, with poetry. His life was in itself a blessing, and Krishna had decided, "This man needs a visit from me."

You can see the story — the man is not at all thinking of Krishna, but Krishna, on his own part, feels that this man deserves a visit. He goes in the middle of the night, so as not to create any trouble in the whole town. He finds the man's door open and he goes in.

The man's mother is very sick, and he is massaging her feet. Krishna comes behind him and says, "I am Krishna and I have come to give you an audience, a *darshana*."

The man said, "This is not the right time; I am massaging my mother's feet."

Meanwhile, just by his side there was a brick; he pushed the brick back — he did not even look back to see who this Krishna is — he pushed the brick and told him to sit down, and that when he was finished with his work he would see him. But he was so much absorbed in massaging the mother's feet — she was almost dying — that the whole night passed, and Krishna remained standing there.

He said, "This is a strange stupidity. People are singing their whole life, `Hare Krishna, Hare Rama' and I never go there. And I have come here and this fool has not even looked back!"

And then it was getting light, the sun was rising, and Krishna became afraid, because people would be coming in. The road was just by the side of the house, and the door was open — and if they saw him standing there, soon there would be trouble, great crowds would come. So he disappeared, leaving just a stone statue of himself on the brick.

When the mother went to sleep, the man turned and said, "Who is the fellow who was disturbing me in the night?" And he found just a statue of Krishna.

The whole village gathered — this was a miracle, what had happened? He told the whole story. They said, "You are a strange fellow. Krishna himself had come, and you are such a fool! You could have at least offered him something to eat, something to drink. He was a guest."

The man said, "At that time there was nothing by my side except this brick. And whenever I am doing something, I do it with totality. I don't want any interference. If he is so much interested in being seen, he can come again, there is no hurry."

That statue remains in the temple of Bitthal, still standing on a brick. But the man was really a great man — not bothering about rewards or anything, absorbed so fully in every action that the action itself becomes the reward. And even if God comes, the reward that is coming out of the totality of action is bigger than God.

Nobody has interpreted the story the way I am interpreting it, but you can see that any other interpretation is nonsense.

So just forget about spirituality, enlightenment, God — they will take care of themselves. That is their business.

They are sitting there without customers, you need not worry. You do the best you can do with life — that is your test, that is your worship, that is your religion. And everything else will follow on its own accord.

The Tea Ceremony
A PRACTICAL GUIDE

THE WAY OF TEA

"In the liquid amber within the ivory porcelain,
the initiated may touch the sweet reticence of Confucius,
the piquancy of Lao Tzu, and the ethereal aroma
of Shakyamuni Buddha himself."
—from The Book of Tea

The traditional Japanese tea ceremony, as it is practiced now, is a complex and elaborate set of rituals. But like any meditation or spiritual practice, if the ritual is given too much emphasis it can easily obscure the original purpose — in this case, to bring meditation and awareness to the most commonplace and humble acts. Elsewhere in this book, Osho has explained the basic elements of the tea ceremony, and the purpose behind it. This small appendix to the book is intended not to spell out details of the traditional ritual, but simply to provide a guide to the basic tools that each reader needs to create his or her own unique tea ceremony.

TOOLS

Many of us might prepare our everyday cup of tea by pouring boiling water over a bag attached to a string — but a truly meditative tea experience opens up a treasure chest

of opportunities for those who love beautiful objects that are also functional. Whether you are drawn to the simplicity and subtlety of the Japanese aesthetic, or the baroque extravagance of your great-grandmother's heirloom china, there is a special delight in using tools that provide not just functionality but also a treat for your senses.

If you don't already have a tea service, take your time in shopping around for one — and make the shopping a meditation, too! Let your eyes lead you to the beautiful, but don't stop there. Pick up a cup, feel its weight and texture. Tap on the side of a pot with your fingernail and listen to the sound. Think of all the little extras that might be useful to have: Do you need a bamboo scoop for the Japanese powdered green tea, or a special container for your favorite herbal blend? How about a silver-plated and filigreed strainer for keeping stray leaves out of your English style "cuppa," or an elegant lacquered tray to accompany the Japanese pot with the bamboo handle? Perhaps you want to think about a special cupboard to store or display your collection, once you've assembled everything you need.

THE INGREDIENTS

"The afternoon glow is brightening the bamboos,
the fountains are bubbling with delight, the soughing
of the pines is heard in our kettle. Let us dream of evanescence,
and linger in the beautiful foolishness of things."
—from The Book of Tea

Apart from herbs, which have been used in different ways for centuries to promote healing, stimulation or relaxation, all of the hundreds of variations of what we call tea come from essentially the same plant, the *Camellia Sinensis*. The plant is indeed a relative of the shrub *Camellia Japonica*, which produces those lovely flowers that are such an important element of so much of classical Japanese painting and textile design.

The differences between teas are the result of differences in where they are grown, how they are harvested, and how the harvest is processed. The finest teas are those where only the most aromatic and tender top two leaves of the leaf bud are used. Producing good tea is a labor-intensive process that can only be done properly by hand, and a single pound of top-grade tea might contain up to 80,000 handpicked leaf buds.

There are four broad categories of tea that emerge out of the different methods of processing the tea leaves, as follows:

WHITE TEAS

As you begin to explore the different qualities and varieties of tea, one of the most treasured varieties you will hear about is called "Silver Needle." The name is appropriate for the tea that comes from this method of harvesting, where leaves are picked at the youngest and most delicate stage, and are still covered with a fine, downy hair. This variety also involves the least processing of the

leaves once they are picked. Usually the harvest is simply steamed and dried, though some varieties might be slightly fermented. Another popular white tea is called White Peony. White teas have a pale yellow color when infused, and a delicate, fresh flavor.

GREEN TEAS

Recent medical studies have shown that not only is green tea a tasty and refreshing way to stay awake during meditation, it also appears to have important beneficial effects on overall health. After picking the green leaves are spread out in the hot air to wither and become softer and more pliable. Traditionally, they are then pan-fried in woks — which prevents the leaves from oxidizing, or fermenting. These leaves are then rolled in one of a variety of ways — twisted, curled, or rolled into balls — which will determine how the tea releases its natural substances and flavor when it is steeped before drinking. Finally, the leaves are dried in a kiln, which stabilizes the fragrance and flavor.

There are many different varieties and qualities of green tea available in the market, and you will want to experiment with different kinds to see what appeals to you. The most common green tea exported from Japan is called Sencha, and the finer qualities of Sencha have a flat, dark green leaf that produces as pleasant and slightly sweet taste. The tea that is used in the formal Japanese Tea Ceremony is called Matcha, which comes in a fine powder and requires special preparation. Matcha is prepared in a

bowl, and traditionally is passed around and shared by the guests in the ceremony. Precise directions for preparation will vary, but basically the Matcha powder is scooped into the bowl, and just enough hot water is added at first to create a thin paste by blending it with a special bamboo whisk. Then more water is added, and the mixture is whisked to create the distinctive foam and soupy consistency that makes this tea such a special treat.

OOLONG TEAS

Most Oolong teas are produced in China and Taiwan (Formosa), and are made from larger, more mature leaves than the green teas. At harvest, the leaves are spread out in direct sunlight until they wither and soften. The leaves are then gathered into bamboo baskets and shaken to bruise the edges, which starts a process of fermentation. After being spread out to dry in a shady place, the process of gathering and shaking the leaves, and then spreading them out to dry, is repeated several times until the leaf edges begin to turn red. The degree of oxidation that is allowed to take place determines whether the tea becomes a "green" oolong (where much of the center of the leaf remains green) or a more classic variety where more than half the leaf is oxidized. Once the desired level is reached, the harvest is pan-fired at high temperatures to halt the fermentation process.

BLACK TEAS

The reason that black teas and oolong teas have until recently been much better known in the West than the green and white teas has to do with transportation and shelf life! Back in the days when tea had to be carried by ship, it was of primary importance to that the leaves be processed in such a way that they would not spoil on the journey.

Black teas (or red teas, as they are sometimes called) are spread out on racks to wither and lose most of their moisture before they are rolled to release their essential oils and juices. After rolling, the leaves are brought inside to a large, cool and humid room where they are spread and allowed to oxidize, darkening the leaf color and allowing the bitter juices to mellow. The oxidation process must be stopped at just the right moment to maximize flavor and aroma, which is achieved by firing the leaves in large ovens.

HERBAL TEAS

Herbs have been used throughout human history to support health, influence mood and vitality, and support relaxation. And one way to extract the various benefits of these herbs is to prepare them in a tea. Nowadays, many commercial varieties and blends of herb teas exist, and some of them offer excellent quality. But you can also experiment with creating your own blends of herbal teas by using different herbs in combination. What follows is a brief guide to some of the most easily obtainable ingredients that are suitable for infusion in teas, and the properties of each. There are many more available — and you will want to find sources for herbs that grow naturally in your own region, which can often bring unique benefits and freshness to your cup.

Astragalus   Supports the immune system, a staple of traditional Chinese and East Indian medicine.

Chamomile   Relaxing, good bedtime tea. Also good to settle upset stomach and other gastrointestinal discomforts. Use leaves and flowers.

Cranberry   Supports the kidneys and helps to prevent recurring urinary tract infections. A good source of Vitamin C. Use crushed, dried berries.

Dandilion   Leaves are a natural diuretic; roots are a mild laxative and support liver function.

Echinacea   Supports the immune system, and can be very effective when taken at the earliest signs of symptoms to prevent or lessen the severity of a cold. Use the leaves or roots.

Feverfew   Good for migraines, fever, menstrual cramps. Not to be taken during pregnancy, and should be used sparingly to avoid gastric disturbances or mouth ulcers. Use the leaves.

Ginger Root	Helpful in easing nausea and upset stomach, and in moderation has a balancing effect on circulation.
Ginseng Root	Invigorating and refreshing, good antidote for tiredness and stress. Avoid during pregnancy or with cardiac disease or hypertension.
Goldenseal Root	Helpful in relieving cold and flu symptoms in the upper respiratory tract. Avoid during pregnancy and lactation, or if you have high blood pressure.
Licorice Root	Good for bronchitis, upper respiratory congestion and stomach ulcers. Stimulates adrenal glands, and is therefore useful in fatigue due to adrenal exhaustion. Not recommended during pregnancy and lactation, and may interfere with hormone therapy.
Passion Flower	Mild sedative effect.
Peppermint	Calms upset stomach and disturbances of the intestinal tract. Also good for inflammation or irritation of the gums.

PREPARING MATCHA TEA

The traditional Japanese tea ceremony usually features the fine powdered green tea known as "Matcha." This powder is also used to flavor sweets and ice creams, and is particularly potent! So it is best not to serve it too close to bedtime. Opposite are step-by-step illustrations for preparing Matcha tea.

1. *As the water is heating on the stove and before it comes to a boil, place one heaping scoop plus one small scoop of Matcha tea powder into a bowl.*

2. *Just before the water comes to a full boil, pour just enough hot water over the powder to make a thin paste when blended with the whisk.*

3. *Add another measure of water and whisk the tea in a gentle circular motion, moving from the bottom of the bowl towards the top of the liquid until a light froth is achieved.*

4. *Present the tea to your guest.*

The traditional Japanese ceremony includes many more steps in an elaborate and graceful ritual that includes "purifying" the bowl and tea scoop by wiping them first with a silk cloth. The bowl and the whisk are then rinsed with hot water and the bowl is dried with a linen cloth before the Matcha powder is added to it. A special jar is used to hold the rinse water.

Guests at a traditional tea ceremony also have certain obligations, such as commenting on the beauty of various implements and art objects in the room.

ABOUT THE AUTHOR

Osho's teachings defy categorization, covering everything from the individual quest for meaning to the most urgent social and political issues facing society today. His books are not written but are transcribed from audio and video recordings of extemporaneous talks given in response to questions from disciples and visitors over a period of 35 years. Osho has been described by the *Sunday Times* in London as one of the "1000 Makers of the 20th Century" and by *Sunday Mid-Day* (India) as one of the ten people — along with Gandhi, Nehru and Buddha — who have changed the destiny of India.

About his own work Osho has said that he is helping to create the conditions for the birth of a new kind of human being. He has often characterized this new human being as "Zorba the Buddha" — capable both of enjoying the earthy pleasures of a Zorba the Greek and the silent serenity of a Gautama the Buddha. Running like a thread through all aspects of Osho's work is a vision that encompasses both the timeless wisdom of the East and the highest potential of Western science and technology.

He is also known for his revolutionary contribution to the science of inner transformation, with an approach to meditation that acknowledges the accelerated pace of contemporary life. His unique "Active Meditations" are designed to first release the accumulated stresses of body and mind, so that it is easier to experience the thought-free and relaxed state of meditation.

ALSO BY OSHO

The Book of Secrets
Osho Zen Tarot
Meditation: The First and Last Freedom
Courage: The Joy of Living Dangerously
Creativity: Unleashing the Forces Within
Maturity: The Responsibility of Being Oneself
Osho Transformation Tarot
Autobiography of a Spiritually Incorrect Mystic
Love, Freedom, and Aloneness
Intuition: Knowing Beyond Logic
Awareness: The Key to Living in Balance
Intimacy: Trusting Oneself and the Other

AUDIO

The Book of Secrets
Osho Meditations on Zen
Osho Meditations on Tao
Osho Meditations on Yoga
Osho Meditations on Buddhism
Osho Meditations on Sufism
Osho Meditations on Tantra

Meditation Resort

OSHO COMMUNE INTERNATIONAL

The Meditation Resort at Osho Commune International has been created by Osho as a place where people can have a direct personal experience of a new way of living with more alertness, relaxation, and fun. Located about 100 miles southeast of Bombay in Pune, India, the resort offers a variety of programs to the thousands of visitors who visit each year from more than 100 countries around the world.

Originally developed as a summer retreat for Maharajas and wealthy British colonialists, Pune is now a thriving modern city that is home to a number of universities and high-tech industries. The Meditation Resort spreads over 32 acres in a tree-lined suburb known as Koregaon Park. Although the resort campus does not provide accommodation for guests, there is a plentiful variety of nearby hotels and private apartments available for stays of a few days up to several months.

Resort programs are all based in Osho's vision of a qualitatively new kind of human being who is able both to participate creatively in everyday life and to relax into silence and meditation. Most programs take place in modern, air-conditioned facilities and include a variety of individual sessions, courses and workshops covering everything from creative arts to holistic health treatments, personal growth and therapy, esoteric sciences, the "Zen" approach to sports and recreation, relationship issues, and significant life transitions for men and women. Both individual sessions and group workshops are offered throughout the year, alongside a full daily schedule of Osho's active meditations, audio and video recordings of his talks, and meditation techniques from a variety of spiritual traditions.

Outdoor cafes and restaurants within the resort grounds serve both traditional Indian fare and a choice of international dishes, all made with organically grown vegetables from the commune's own farm. The campus has its own private supply of safe, filtered water.

Acknowledgments

Photos on pages xii, 7, 27 and 60 by Sidd Murray-Clarke
All others courtesy of Osho International, New York

Details of photos from the Meditation Resort at Osho
Commune International, Pune, India, are as follows:
Page XV, 16, 47, 50, 79, 81: Lao Tzu Garden
Page 13: Rock garden near Osho Café
Page 23: Lotus Pond near Osho Multimedia offices,
    Mirdad Building
Pages 29, 54, 96, 98: Osho Teerth Ecological Zen Garden
Page 34: Welcome Center garden pond
Page 42: Meditation workshop in the Dojo
Pages 55-56: Overview and architectural detail
    of the resort's Pyramid complex of facilities
Page 64: Rock garden near Creative Arts complex
Page 77: Tree accommodation near the boutique
Page 85: Path outside Buddha Auditorium

Page 1: The Zen story quoted appears in the book, *ZEN
BUDDHISM: AN INTRODUCTION TO ZEN (With Stories,
Parables and Koan Riddles told by the Zen Masters, with Cuts
from old Chinese Ink-Paintings.)* Reprinted with permission
from Peter Pauper Press, Inc., White Plains, NY.

For More Information

For information about visiting the resort in India,
or to learn more about Osho and his work, see:

www.osho.com

A comprehensive web site in different languages, featuring
an on-line tour of the Meditation Resort, books and tapes,
a list of Osho information centers worldwide, and
selections from Osho's talks.

OSHO INTERNATIONAL
New York
email: **osho-int@osho.com**